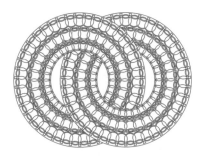

SERAPHIM

SERAPHIM

ANGELIQUE ZOBITZ

CAVANKERRY PRESS

CavanKerry Press Ltd.
Fort Lee, New Jersey
www.cavankerrypress.org

Publisher's Cataloging-in-Publication Data
provided by Five Rainbows Cataloging Services
Names: Zobitz, Angelique, author. | Acosta, Grisel Y., writer of foreword.
Title: Seraphim / Angelique Zobitz ; foreword by Dr. Grisel Y. Acosta.
Description: Fort Lee, NJ : CavanKerry Press, 2024.
Identifiers: ISBN 978-1-960327-04-8 (paperback)
Subjects: LCSH: Women—Poetry. | Women, Black—Poetry. | Mothers and daughters—Poetry. | Intersectionality (Sociology)—Poetry. | Social justice—Poetry. | Poetry. | BISAC: POETRY / American / African American & Black. | POETRY / Subjects & Themes / Political & Protest. | POETRY / Women Authors.
Classification: LCC PS3626.O63 S47 2024 (print) | DDC 811/.6—dc23.

Cover and interior text design by Mayfly Design
First Edition 2024, Printed in the United States of America

 Made possible by funds from the
New Jersey State Council on the Arts, a partner
agency of the National Endowment for the Arts.

CavanKerry Press is grateful for the support it receives from the
New Jersey State Council on the Arts.

In addition, CavanKerry Press gratefully acknowledges generous
emergency support received during the COVID-19 pandemic
from the following funders:

The Academy of American Poets
Community of Literary Magazines and Presses
National Book Foundation
New Jersey Arts and Culture Recovery Fund
New Jersey Council for the Humanities
New Jersey Economic Development Authority
Northern New Jersey Community Foundation
The Poetry Foundation
US Small Business Administration

Also by Angelique Zobitz

Love Letters to The Revolution (2020)
Burn Down Your House (2021)

To the Seraphim,

but most especially my mother—

Katrina Page (1964–2023)

The name Seraphim clearly indicates their ceaseless and eternal revolution about Divine Principles, their heat and keenness, the exuberance of their intense, perpetual, tireless activity, and their elevative and energetic assimilation of those below, kindling them and firing them to their own heat, and wholly purifying them by a burning and all-consuming flame; and by the unhidden, unquenchable, changeless, radiant, and enlightening power, dispelling and destroying the shadows of darkness.

—Dionysius the Areopagite, *The Celestial Hierarchy*

Contents

Foreword

When you grow up as an Afro-Latinx punk artist outsider, you get used to your peripheral role in the world. You go in and out of the centers of many spaces, but where you live is beyond. You have a celestial view of all your spaces and see how they interrelate, but many of your peers live in just one of these spaces and do not necessarily see you as an integral part of them. You come to expect looks of shock when you decide to place yourself in the spotlight of one space. Or, you come to welcome those advantageous moments when no one sees you at all. You will remember that overt rejection will come again. "Why doesn't anyone get my references to Time Zone's 'World Destruction'?" you'll cry out. Or, at yet another boring meeting of some kind, you'll mention how everyone in the room could benefit from reading Izumi Suzuki, knowing full well they won't look her up. You will expect someone to exert power, authority, even violence. You will learn to fearlessly be yourself regardless. However, you do *not* allow yourself to ever expect to meet someone else who lives on the periphery, because it is too rare to hope for it. It is too serendipitous to expect to meet someone who knows what it means to whip in and out of different cultural spaces, literary spaces, musical spaces, ethnic and racial spaces, and differently gendered spaces. It's fine; you know you are in the minority and have come to accept that fact. Not everyone lives in a liminal space and that's okay. It takes all kinds. So, you can understand how surprised I was upon reading the work of

Angelique Zobitz, and how surprised I was to recognize so much within the pages of *Seraphim*.

Zobitz is writing to the fiercest of angels, women who raised her, who lived with her, and who inspire her. This intimate conversation invokes the work of other women who write directly to their communities, women like Keisha-Gaye Anderson and Cynthia Manick. However, there is an edge, surely influenced by her punk rock mother and her own explorations into deviating from the norm. She writes in "Kink Therapy, or An Alternate History of the World":

> For need of bread there were days where I slid a noose
> around the necks of White
> men, put my boots in their backs, and watched the brown
> skin of my knuckles pull
> taut while I: composed my grocery list, considered the
> aubergine paint of my nails.

Zobitz points to the gendered problems in our economic system, reverses race-based colonial hierarchy, uses these themes within an empowered female role, and does this all with a booted, deviant, dry humor wink. Lines like these, so rich and dense with the context I mention, invite the reader to see this normally hidden world as more complex than they might imagine. After pleasing a client with the "unspeakable," the narrator wonders what exactly is reflected by this exchange, concluding, "the opposite of a mirror still doesn't have a name."

Not surprisingly, because of the title, much of this work is rooted in religious motifs. Angels abound, but so do gods, prayer, and otherworldly realms. The motifs are used to tie the poems together, not proselytize. In fact, several of the poems reveal the tension of being female under religion. An epigraph of long-distance runner Steve Prefontaine leads us into the complex parallels between childbirth and child beatings. In "Because You Need to Learn," the narrator is counseled to pray about devilish trauma, but instead decides that fighting is better. Nearly every poem has language rooted in some aspect of religion. Normally, as a preacher's kid myself, this would be off-putting, as I've had enough of that in my life, but the unexpected juxtapositions are a delight. The camp factor of "A Mouth Full of Prayers for Wendy Williams" alone is enough for a belly laugh, but when we get to, "Praise her resilience. / She could love a man who: // brought back another baby, / set up two households" in the poem, our image of Williams has shifted, and rightly so. By the time we read "After Listening to Roberta Flack Singing 'Angelitos Negros,'" one of a series of ekphrastic poems based on music, equating our female heroes with angels becomes utopic. We hear the "radiant warmth of their words" found "in the sweet succor of another's laughter," and we know the world feels right in these moments. Angels, indeed.

On Earth, however, if these angels take on physical bodies, they will not be seen as the holy creatures they are; they will be seen as something dangerous that needs to be either subjugated or destroyed. The poem, "This Country Will Require You to Be Magical, Then Attempt to Burn You for Being a Witch" exemplifies this idea. It extends it to the burdensome concept of Black Girl Magic, which doesn't allow a full range of human emotion to be exhibited by Black women. No one wants to be or can be magical all the time, and it is horrible to have that expectation. Zobitz writes:

> Girl-child, power-in-waiting, Revolution,
> this world will try to cleave you
> in half, reach inside—
> lay waste, leave you
> a bloody mess of seed . . .

While the poem may start with the pain of the problem, she reminds the reader that, as a witch, the power is in her hands: "burn them down—/ teach them our bodies / are best left alone." This kind of ending points to José Estéban Muñoz's concept of the queer utopic, where he claims that queerness is not rooted in the present but in a utopic future, or what could be seen on the horizon by folks who can see possibilities. As I mentioned at the beginning of this introduction, my own existence is rooted in being on the periphery and having a bird's-eye view of many worlds, and Muñoz captures the superpower of this perspective. It is a fierce and hopeful one. Zobitz's words in this poem predict a world where "witches" (meaning women and queer folk, to me) are finally left alone because the larger community finally recognizes our power. They do not burn or beat us out of fear anymore; they leave us alone out of awe. That is utterly utopic and I'm here for it.

What I am also here for, as someone born and raised in Chicago, are all the Chi-Town references, whether they are an allusion to Harold's Chicken Shack, via a three-piece, or the winter hawk, or Wild Irish Rose, or North Halsted bars. I grew up in Logan Square but went to high school in Hyde Park, so I had friend groups on the North, South, and West Sides of Chicago but there are very few people who regularly travel between the areas. They usually stick to one part of the city. It is rare that I read a text rooted in Chicago that has references to spaces far and wide in the city. We see our beloved hometown within a resurrection narrative in "These are the mysteries of my faith," where the frosty winter months represent death, a grandmother's biscuits represent rebirth, and waiting for a lover represents the hopeful return. She writes, "No one could measure love without the cup— / the way she did. Her arthritis-knotted fingers / . . . transformed into heaven."

We revisit the power of a recipe in "Black Bodies," where Black folks "debate the deliciousness / of banana pudding with Nilla / versus Chessmen," and the "Yo mama" tradition is transformed into something just as sublime as a centuries-old, family-made dessert. Zobitz creates a similar recipe in two poems that ground the collection in the voices that inform it. Two centos, titled

"Love Letter to The Revolution No. 1" and "Love Letter to The Revolution No. 2," use the words of bell hooks, Ntozake Shange, Lucille Clifton, Sonia Sanchez, Gwendolyn Brooks, and Audre Lorde, among many other greats. These angels are the ingredients used for Zobitz's craft, and the result is something we can both have and have nourish us. It requires a complex palate, and it requires time to digest. Enjoy that time; savor it. This is a rare experience brought to you by a unique voice that has its roots in many places. Many of its branches will seem familiar, but it is in the woven combination of these branches that we will see the unfamiliar, the strange but very welcome voice that will enlighten us and perhaps give us a glimpse of heaven.

Dr. Grisel Y. Acosta
September, 2023

you are your mother's child

Sister/Seraphim, Inextinguishable Light

They dancing and singing tonight.

Black Barbies backlit by gas station fluorescence

stunning—singing holy, holy, holy.

Their loud praises rattling my window,
syncopated steps, wings out, rhythm on, radiant
with the backbeat unbroken, backs unbroken,
unfettered and unbothered in eight and sixteen time.

This very night there before me is an angel and
I saw her drop it low.

All while cars pull in and out,
top off, or fill up at the pumps—
I can relate to being half empty
and thirsting to be full.

She—her—they—they blazing.

This could be worship.
Loud and exuberant as every light-

leached club where I once got hot and sweaty
to reggae, rubbed underneath some body
as vigorously as kindling before catching fire.

It could be easy to forget how
good adoration feels (I can't forget),
what good feels like (paradise).

They so flame and I see it.

It could be heaven.
This lot of half-leveled bumpy concrete
glittering full jeweled with bottle shards and
wrapping paper confetti.

They could burn it all down.
But—Glory.

They invite us to join the chorus.

Angelique, an Origin Story

My mama said, I was blessed born. Said, she didn't need divine
messenger to convince her of what she carried, knew immediately

that I didn't need to be brought into this world by virgin or conceived

as sacrifice. Didn't need a sign—she knew a good thing coming,
despite the short-term trouble for a teen nearly as young as Mary.

She'd already done a lot of living in her small corner of the world.

My mama said, her mama said, and really because my people say
there's power in names, like the many names of God—one of which

has got to be mama or also like we say *name it and claim it* or like

when you're reaching for a word like moist or itch no other
word will do—all that got her thinking.

My mama said when they laid me to her breast, she cradled me to her
chest where her beating heart hummed of survival and salvation, and

that throbbing tune lulled us both to sleep. My mama said, a punk

girl can dream of angels and know when one manifests.
She said she looked into an angel's eyes and claimed it as her own.

Love Letter to The Revolution No. 1

Little Sister,

Nobody spoke to me about the moon.
or how

to fashion a world that will hold all the people
these stains & scars are mine.

So—

I will give you thunder / shatter your hearts
with rain / let snow soothe you / make your

healing water / clear sweet—
teach you to:

laugh and dance and sing and / play and drink
their wine and religion and success

and outlast.

Come celebrate / with me that everyday /
something has tried to kill me / and has failed.

And you are your mother's child.
Be who you are and will be / learn to cherish /

that boisterous Black Angel that drives you.
Picture the daylight / bringing her to woods /

full of birth moons

There you are.

Grocery Shopping, Ars Poetica

age 15

"Baby. Put that one back,"
my grandmother
takes the unripened
watermelon from my hand,

places it back on the shelf, rolls it over,
shows me that the bare patch
where it dirt rested isn't the light

green of fecundity.
Asks me to press against the fruit—
"too soft," she tsks,
then thumps against the rind,

"can you hear that dullness?"
She says, "What's ripe
is sturdy and has resonance,
produces a satisfying sound."

She teaches me what it means
to be bursting with juice
ready to be devoured.

age 20

I enter with eyes
bigger than my mouth.
I want it all. My need
is greater than want.

I want to fill up my cart
full to the brim,
overfill this vessel with all
I can get my hands on. Yet,

there's only so much
space. What goes or
stays is a matter of taste,
planning, execution.

What is left
consumes me
becomes me.

age 35

The offerings are plenty.

What does it cost me—
the items I carry?

I must learn
to choose carefully.

Lay each on the table.
Expose what's damaged

to scrutiny and light.

Because You Need to Learn

Somebody may beat me, but they are going to have to bleed to do it.
—Steve Prefontaine

I.

Born on the cusp between winter and rain,
I took control of my mother's young body,

grasped handfuls of her insides, held tight and recalcitrant.
I struck my fist against her uterus walls,

reconstructed her function to fit my form,
until I broke every rib, popped every tendon in the hip joints,

touched her in the head, and resentful of this round's rousing,
I staged a last stand,

cooled her down and burned her up,
refused to run.

Big Ma demanded of the doctor—
get that child out tonight.

I was heaved into midnight—with old seeing eyes,
the proud point of an elfin chin,

independent perambulation,
a mouth that was already too fond of running.

I heard Big Ma's strong voice declare me a changeling child,
she beseeched my mother to send me to Deep South relatives

where the madness would not be catching.

Years later, a former friend,
raised junkyard mad, tail fast as Friday night,

knocked out my two front teeth for
no other reason than the love of her young life held my hand—

I ambled down the gridlines of city blocks to Aunt Quince's house,
wind whistling by my ear, sturdy arms flailing,

a soup of tears, snot, and blood smeared
across the top lip, baby teeth left to the concrete,

each step overpronating, my stomach heaving,
what I would not find was pity or comfort

surrounded by the six sepia-toned faces of the play cousins
who loved me best and well, *fight her or fight us*:

—so
I did.

As tears flowed down my cheeks, I won in every sloppy fist
that bounced off her less than blameless cheek—apology

in every *i. did. not. want. to. do. this. but. you. made. me.*
as I rained down as cold as the cusp,

a changeling child who turned her mother mad.

II.

A child that never learned her place, I lost my innocence
in every impeccably aimed corrective fist Uncle Eddie laid down.

I would go for his eyes but the backhand across my mouth
echoed down to my toes, the bitch slap tilted my head high,

arched my back concave then convex
before the inelegant crash landing

on the rain slick metal door hinge.
He would sneer, *Stop crying*

before I give you something to cry about.
I learned to slowly collect my broken body

from the sidewalk, swallow back the pain,
and not utter the bitter words.

The ragged edges of the gaping wound less
painful than the secrets buried under cover of midnight.

My Black flesh became accustomed to collecting
physical wounds like misbegotten merit badges.

After the first scab tore, oozed pus and blood
under the yellow and burgundy gold of my school jumper,

I developed perfect posture, because a quickly healed scar
was reprieve.

Gangly arms, knock-kneed, and bucktooth,
hail stones and thunder buried in my breastbone,

I attempted to bottle it away.
Sister Barbara counseled me to pray,

to remember the transitory nature of my suffering,
but for every switch I picked, u-shaped welt too tender

to touch, my silent suffering buffered
a rage as prickly as the rose bush switch that tore my skin.

Please understand the reason I pulled the sharpest knife
from the drying rack—I could not take another

I hit you because you need to learn.
The echo sent me back two hundred years,

when they flayed my back wide for running.
In that life, I learned I could not flee the pain,
I had to fight.

I was born on the cusp between hard winter and soft rain.

Kink Therapy, or
An Alternate History of the World

For need of bread there were days where I slid a noose around the necks of White men, put my boots in their backs, and watched the brown skin of my knuckles pull taut while I: composed my grocery list, considered the aubergine paint of my nails, calculated the tipping point between asphyxiation and role play.

I rode their backs, the miserable beasts, made these men into collared horses who carried my burdens, dug my heels into their lathered flesh, shamed them into the ground. *Are you so weak that you can't carry the burden of one Black woman?* Once I chained a man ankle to wrist over the spanking bench and with the strategic application of medical grade lubricant forced him to take what I would give.

My favorite client had impeccable manners, a sweet thank you for every bruise. My bare foot firmly rubbed across the freckled cream skin of his cheek flushed him red as spring roses. He was allowed to come on Saturdays and brought me tins of coffee: Harar, Caturra, Kona, Pacamara, Arusha, Sumatra, Mayagüez, Sulawesi Toraja, Kalossi, Catimor, Timor, Bonifieur, Yirgacheffe, Uganda.

He only asked for what I formerly considered unspeakable acts. He begged me to beat his guilt away, to be tethered to a table, the Saint Andrew's cross, or the ceiling. I told him to repeat after me—*I ain't shit* and *I mean nothing*—compelled him to make ape sounds while he masturbated at whip point, tears flecked his flushed cheeks. He sought absolution and I spoke reparations. I told him to let it go. And he came and I came to the conclusion, the opposite of a mirror still doesn't have a name.

Yearning Is Prayer Without an Addressee

Breathing   is   longing.

What better   illustration   is   there

                     than

to

     be   without

          and   want

                                    for

          fulfillment—

than   to   be   an   empty   lung

                          gasping

          for

                                    air?

Full Throated

You must be thinking of my grandma's people.

Must have me confused
with someone else.
I see the resemblance.
But I'm not the one,

won't be

compelled to cradle
every word on my tongue
behind the caging of my
teeth only birthing

Black ass bon mot babies
for your pleasure.

Bite my tongue?
I've heard, *hold your peace,*
and requests that I stay calm
and maintain the illusion of peace.

(Recall, we're all happy
if we're quiet.)

Bitch,
please.

My people trapped sharp
words in the esophagus,
dulled them down on the concrete
slabs of solitary confinement,

sacrificed in silence
while carving in the throat

I was here

bold subversive graffiti
scrawled in the night.

The fumes of their words are why
my throat is dry from how often
I refuse to choke gag reflex
fix my mouth.

If you only knew what
I want to say when you utter
temper your temper

as if a soft word makes palatable misery
as if tongue separates the bitter from sweet
as if it is my party trick to swallow back the bitter pit
as if tying my anger into knots like a cherry stem—

Woo—ma'am!
Bless.

I am not my grandma's—

child, that generation put
up with what they had to.

I never learned how to sweet
and swallow bad produce.

To fix my lips for long,
never rouged them red,
in replacement of bloodlust.

I too want words
soft on skin soft on psyche
lapping softly in my inner
ear revolutionary love words,

like: *you matter.*

Until then
I let sing,
every word.

Till It Moves Like a Slow Song Sounds

after Patricia Smith

Friday

My great-auntie used to hold me till
police sirens crept down the street—we'd feel it

go silent, quiet—thrumming in alleyways. Her rough hand moves
up and down and across my back, from nape to blade like

cat foot smooth steppers at the lounge clasping hands in a
prayer of what we find holy, Al Green crooning slow

molasses rhythm, soul communion, skin to skin carrying a song
as she crafted love out of terror sounds.

Saturday

For every stovetop press and curl Joyce held my head still
Friday night liquor fumes wafting near my nose, sometimes she hit
my ear, I'd flinch at the hot comb sizzle—how fast my straight back moves
in that vinyl-covered seat. She'd tap my shoulder with her hand still silent like
we both learned to not say *I'm sorry* when others hurt us in a-
roundabout way, watching her ex-husband walk late and slow
through the door, no hurry to pick up the boys she raised: while a song
testifying of what can and cannot be changed sounds.

Sunday

After Mass, I'd lean into the padded kneeler, hand clasped till
I'd run out of adolescent prayers of intercession. Candlelit
incense and taper flames under the rafters move
the Holy Spirit glow over my slick Blue Magic-sheened scalp like

20

every Black saint framed in stained glass above gave benediction, a larghissimo duet—communion of past and present as easy as slow sanctification, soft affection back for every prayer in their names, song as sweet as altar wine and praise and glory without making sounds.

Mame Coumba Bang Speaks to The Revolution

> *She was here before religion,*
> *before Islam, before Christianity. She was here.*
> —*Senegalese legend*

You were born from legend, dear child.
The fishermen learned of us first—

before plunder, before thirst, before
baptism, before suckling at breast,

there was me and you nestled in me.
Formed first from salt and undertow

in my watery womb, you a caviar
in my fleshy belly born in the sweet mouth

of the river. You walked on water before men,
you fish and loaves, called for offerings, given milk

in droves. The sailors, travelers, foreigners learned
to behave with gratitude, else risk drowning.

There was no god with dominion that made
us goddess, who chooses what you will accept.

Seek not oblivion or rest, stop wading only
to walk the night as deceptive and dangerous

as the river ready to take more than you need.

we sang the stars

Transfiguration,
or As the Spirit Is, So Follows the Body

At night, The Revolution and I
deliberate the benefits of metamorphosis,
the merits of inhabiting animal bodies,

consider the gifts, and settle that to be a bird of prey
swivel necked, keen eyed, with crushing
beak and claw—a great horned owl would be best.

We discuss whether we subsist
only on crow or snake or juicy mouse or frog.
Question if it's more fulfilling to crunch the bone

or chew the rubber band tendons until they snap
under the pressure of our attention
than to peel the skin back and chew warm

and pulpy the muscles of coldblooded beasts.
You know I've eaten frog and snake, yeah mama?
But mice and crow, I suppose I'd learn to love the taste.

She nods her head and snuggles into my body.
To her I am the fiercest, hungriest animal.
It is so tender and good.

What is truth but what we have all agreed to believe?

A Mouth Full of Prayers for Wendy Williams

I.

What woman hasn't been bent
back from her self, skinned down
to interior muscle left, an exposed
shell contaminated with specks of dirt?
An oyster cracked open early ugly
vulnerable, ready to misshapen, pearl.
Who hasn't borne flawed love
just to call themselves loved, to see
love in the sentence next to their names,
accepting half of what could be whole
because at least you are not alone?
Gal, listen.

II.

He only comes with need
beds built of magnolia buds
your back ink tilled dusk

III.

to him you are a little whisper only
uttered at night yet, *persistence* as
long as you can cradle a lie in your
thighs and call it a home for when
he comes back.

That sound.

IV.

Don't lie. We've all suffered second-
guessing the motives of his missing
when you needed him most.

V.

Beloved,

I wrote   long(ing less) distance

letters to [the] love   of my young life
that went unanswered   published
writings   I clipped   for him
to read   highlighted   pages of astrological readings
of our future   (which of us needed convincing?)

his reply:
I   am sorry
I   don't respond
I   can't afford distractions

Sincerely.

VI.

Cousin prioritized making him a plate
so he knew she'd be willing to eat
the scraps of his feast.

VII.

Too.
Auntie got a story.

Praise her resilience.
She could love a man who:

brought back another baby,
set up two households in adjacent
states, drove her to drink,

can transform self-hate into complaints,
opinions so ugly they manifest all that bold
obscurification that she's been not enough
enough can't find better not equipped to sing
any song but bitch aint loved anyone half as much
as him who's loving her half as much as deserved until

we all consider it truth.

IIX.

Exhortation: […]

Dust to Bones

I.

Your mother carried love like contraband—
bundled in butcher paper, standing at bus corners,
she offered you a glimpse of what could be had for a price.

II.

No one knows how you do
bitter cold paper-thin skin
blood like water sugar and grits

III.

You looked the most like your father.
It's no wonder he loved you least.
It's hard to make eyes at someone you hate.

IV.

Insensate and wasting away,
you were tied to the bed
when you gouged at the nurses'
faces like a manic sculptor
possessed with scraping away excess.

You begged me for release,
asked me to make different mistakes.

After you recovered, we pretended
I never heard you—as natural as breathing.

V.

You could hear the slaps through the walls—
couldn't take the songs of the babies crying,
their mother crying, the memory of your mother
crying, how it felt when you were crying.

After long nights of gathering your strength
you walked up the stairs and demanded
the neighbors stop fighting.

He cut his eyes but dropped his fist.
You said, *if I wasn't sick, I'd beat your ass.*

VI.

In the store, your grandchildren get lost in
name brands and designer shoes while you sit
praying for strength, writing checks to pay for the past.

Black Marie-Antoinette

*I was a queen, and you took away my crown; a wife, and
you killed my husband; a mother, and you deprived me of my children.
My blood alone remains: take it, but do not make me suffer long.*

—apocryphally attributed to Marie-Antoinette

When you come for me
if I'm making dinner,
let me put the knives
gently to the side—
and turn off the pots
to write my note,
to whoever claims
my abandoned home,
that supper is ready
and to continue
without me.

When you come for me,
give me time to don
my wedding dress,
braid peonies into my hair;
I will leave my vows
on the dressing table
so that my love letters
find a courier
to carry them
forward, a river,
to eternity.

When you come for me,
I will hum
my babies' lullaby—
a hopeful tune
that filled our house
under cover of dark,
and inside the light
we sang the stars
until each beat
bore aching witness.

After Listening to Roberta Flack Singing "Angelitos Negros"

Have you heard the seraphs singing early
on Christmas morning? Seen them watching

the news—eyes alert for signs, or invoking
the Lord's name while soaking their feet

in epsom salt baths?

Have you seen them laughing
at the card table, each hard-fought book

made at spades, proof of good fortune?
I've seen universes in every brown

curve of their celestial bodies, in every
radiant warmth of their words, starlight

peeking out in a game of hide and seek.
I hear them in the sweet succor of another's laughter.

I've been held to the bosom of night—
love poured on me like manna till morning.

The Cardinal and the Camels

We once went wild with night frenzy.

The wafting scent of honeysuckle and love
come and gone. The cockabug brambles never
meant to touch innocent skin sunk into us.

Our dances were pagan.
The natural undulation of snakes and worms.

We swayed with the air and became tipsy off the moon
and in June—the wet set of our feet against gritty sand
at the lake, was heaven despite what was taught in Sunday school.

I remember capturing flickering stars.
And calling them "fireflies." Their loss of luminescence
deeply mourned, having not known the importance of
concepts like love and air—and the care
one must take with both.

We circle danced shaded by the branches of the old oak,
its arms dripped with honeyed wheat,
and the last cardinal I'd ever seen left in the spring
and never returned.

How we snuck the pack of Camels.
That first puff of nicotine,
the burning eyes and the surprise of the burn—
mingled with our briny tears and we all thought

we had sinned. Mortally.

The greedy plucking and suckling
of tart blackberries is long ago.

No magic potion or miracle formula cause the trees
to grow thick and the grape vines to tangle so
the time elapse has grown skewed—
the years are fast, the days are slow.

On Sundays We Were All-American

We:
a) quick-serviced our service and went to first Mass for our
    1-hr-or-less-while-you-wait-God.
b) sign of the cross, stand, sing, genuflect, kneel, stand again,
    sit, daydream.
c) and also with you'ed.

We:
a) footballed. Hard.
b) shouted at the first down.
c) believed in the McMahon, the Dent, and the Payton. 1985
    Da Bears, world without end. Amen.

We:
a) kids on the cusp of blossoming snuck beers and got loose.
b) deep house'd with Mr. Fingers and Frankie Knuckles. "Can
    You Feel It?"
c) front stoop sit.

We:
a) fired up the backyard barbeque.
b) meatloaf-ed, creamed corn, and smothered potatoes.
c) sifted Swan's Down Cake Flour and spun sugar and spice
    into apple pie.

We:
a) subscribed to our side of machine politics.
b) girded ourselves for Monday.
c) knew all of Chicago was burning.

Pyriscence

*for Breonna, Oluwatoyin, Rekia, Riah, Kayla, Dominique,
Michelle, Nina, Miriam, Sandra, Atatiana, Monica, Charleena,
Chynal, Korryn, India, Alexia, Mya, Tanisha, Sheneque, Natasha,
Tanisha, Kendra, LaTanya, Danette, Muhlaysia, Margaret, Dana,
Eleanor, Bee Love, Frankie Ann, Alberta, Tarika, Aiyana, Bailey,
Shereese, Sharmel, Alesia, Shelly, and all the ones we have not
learned of #SayHerName*

/

every tree is potential kindling is potential fire is
potentially a lodgepole pine seed sealed tight with resin
and can only be opened after calefaction has broken
it apart. We can't go into the woods and come out the
other side untouched by brambles or brush fire, are not a
dandelion seed outfitted with parachute free to float and
grow where we land. We are Black Women, therefore we
are often tough seed or tree or strange fruit or kindling.
Adaptation drives us to serotiny, dormant, awaiting
release, blossoming and dying from heat.

//

37

are ███████████████ strange fruit ██████ ████████████████████████████████████ awaiting
release, blossoming and dying from heat.

///

██████████████████████████

████████████████████████████████

██████████████████████████████

████ We ██████████████████████████

███████████████████████████████████

████████████████████████████████

██████████████ Black Women ██████████
are ███████████████████████████████

█████████████████████████████

████████████████ dying from heat.

If you've ever visited a Pentecostal tent revival, then you know

despite a deep fear of
burning a young, sanctified girl somewhere was rocking
an Anita Baker hairstyle and hoping to impress
the pastor. Convince him she's good enough
for his son, even while the grown folk
is whispering about her sexing him
up like his agency was subsumed
by hers. As if she alone is sexual.
Temptress. Devil. Delilah.
Jezebel in knee-length
polyester
like
my young
ears couldn't hear the way
envy spiraled like a fresh press
and curl past my shoulder blades in
bounty. The old men's guilty postures
and the trembling rage in the old women
who missed all that young, furtive, fumbling,
excited, loving, fucking. All of them wishing and
forgetting he was waiting for a moment to be let free
and saved by someone who was braver than judgment
so he could be baptized into new.

My Mama's Got Her GED in Existentialism and Human Emotion

Church is only open on Sunday.

Don't keep asking that God find a way.
God has his hustles in a row.
Out doing something.
here. (I'm making this up)

Jesus still got that black bag.
Julian said
Lawyers said.

People in jail want somebody to love too.
Child love knows—
Upstate, New God knows

Getting head, cake, shots
He go down. But baby—

come dressed to give

Ain't a Bible that has that kind of language.
Don't beg. Give it good.

He didn't do anything.

Look at them.
Is Jesus smiling?

You can't keep asking Jesus to
do things for you,
God is tired of you clapping and laughing.
Where is God?
God said, White people don't live
like God would do.

Everybody said:
Dick said.
And they hadn't done a damned thing.

Grandmother, mother, and daughter
gimme, gimme, gimme, us.
What's God?

bad body, money, and Girl!
Wait for Jesus to pull his pants up

all of them want.

They stand up and you drop to your knees,
crying

And that's why—I tell you Church

Look at Jesus.
Not in one picture.

imperfect yet unbroken

God: The Father

Poor little Catholic girl—
you've given up on calling for your father.

What is God but an absentee father?

Because Father is the name for Daddy
when His presence is felt but He's never seen.

That makes Father a synonym for Faith.

Both are why you stopped calling
on God, having learned He only

made you to sing His praises.

Confession

I want to be a poem
and pried wide open.

Be held by a lover,
who wants to linger.

No one's ever adored me
just for existing, or run

their fingers across my spine
with reverence, spent

themselves analyzing my
edges. I long to be read

at dusk, as soft and earnest
as vesper psalms put

to song. I want to be eased
into, poured over, studied

in rumpled bedsheets,
touched by sleepy fingers

on Sunday morning,
handled as gently as artifact.

After Listening to Megan Thee Stallion's "Thot Shit"

Never had a chance to miss what I never had,
I've spent my time lounging in unmade beds
wrecked by meaningless sex, men I just met—

good girls
don't get good head.

Choir—

for every uttered *that ho over there,*
I consoled myself with no regrets
for the never done or never said.

Exhausted myself in tantric positions,
been held wide open split, molten and volcanic
spent myself between him, her, and them

felt alive and divine,
yes, I did that.

Church—

the one who dipped clever
fingers into my crevices hunting
for a bit of honey, suckled at my
clitoris, and said I tasted of wild
honeysuckle ripe for plucking.

Yes, I've been fucking.

Tongue twisters twisted between
the bodies of men and women,
drunk and eager, phone calls and frenzy.

I've spilt plenty of liquor in North Halsted bars,
littered Lincoln Park with a body count
that didn't heed the warning of my red

pumps and skintight shirts advertising:
Catholic girls do it better.

Aide-Memoire

I am falling back on the familiar comforts—black-eyed
peas with ham hocks, coquito, mango and sticky rice,
crave to eat heat, forget that my stomach has grown
maladapted to the richness of such food, feel stomach
pains to connect with my yam and sharecropping roots,
eat roots, but first fill my belly with hot bowls of grits
or cornbread and collard greens, pig tails sucked down
to the bone, pot liquor broth, full of flavor drank until
the ancestors vibrate a tuning fork to my teeth.

I am surprised by the urge to clean deeply,
purge, winnow, and thwart the encroachment of dust, fix
roots, ward off evil, clean the house with Florida water,
tired of not tasting air, cleanse the corners, the patch-
work rug sprinkled in glitter spills, the wiry shed hair
of the black Lab who finds delight in rolling across the floor.
I am thrumming with restlessness, frantic as the child
who leads and expects us to follow. I open all the windows,
degrease every inch of the stove, clean like our lives depend
on it, mop as if blessings will be found near baseboards.

I find myself speaking roots, a miniature of my mother,
humming old r&b tunes, jill and erykah wailing out for sweet
as summer rain, lush as grass, croons as sticky and salty as taffy.
The air is pungent as honeysuckle, as salty as blues, is sweat
within the juncture of my thighs, d'angelo crying how does it feel—
sinuous affirmation that the body is flesh imperfect yet unbroken
here now made for slow soft worship, good and worthy as gospel
resilient as negro spirituals sung next to the one you love.

For Gods

for Vainis Aleksa

In hushed states we speak of you, still like water in moonlight.
Tranquil in that restless state, the flurry of activity under the lake—
that belies the stillness of the façade. Still waters run deep,
deeper than the words we cut to describe.
Such is the search of making them bleed, soul onto paper.

Remember then that there was only you, the wife,
all five of the kids, up at the cabin. The late rides at night,
eating up air to make it to another place you call home.
Your realm takes you across here to there, other countries,
the roots into still with you.

But now there's glued macaroni stuck in your hair and you don't
care.
And you'll love when she's dirty and he's moody just because.

Did you even imagine?

Your children breathe history: mythologies and pagan beginnings,
small reckonings and large reorganizations. Jogaila married
Poland's queen.
Yet Dievas continued to hold the throne. Perkunas brings forth
more courage
than Custer's last stand, but then there's nothing
like being on the giving end of a stone axe to the head.
That's more Old World, South Side, and sincere than all that is
known. But Saule, Menulis . . .

Here is the most difficult grammatical rule:
do it all with feeling. Make sure to squeeze out the essence of the thing.
It is the execution of an object's essence that is its proper arrangement.
The classes of words, their inflections, their functions and relations
in the sentence only exist because you cause them to;
the way you capture drama, will qualities of moonbeams in dreams,
extol the virtues of marriage, will precede syntax or intelligibility.

On Olympus. We who are high.

Recall the rippled waves of skipped stones and the three different ways
the arm aches before you can go back home. There isn't much to
    remember
except the sun grew low long before the silver bow of the moon rose
to greet half-mast but you kept on floating across the surface of the
    water.

Waiting for the edge of your father's anger to wear off, you piss drunk
    on sweetwater,
peach brandy, fly paper gin, Night Train, and Wild Irish Rose, you
    Mad Dog,
know the history I'm talking about.

He "sent you to school to get a book education" and you lay lounging
    on the lake
with the same friends you know you'll eventually leave behind—them
    with the moonshine,
pool hall, late night brawls—you, who were accustomed to the fight,
    the roughness,
the sensuous caress of life, would grow more mature though not like
    your father.
Neither Kronos nor Zeus. But more a man.

This is evolution.

The consistent chase of the earth rotating on its axis and its silent
    revolution.

Funny how we can say we're in the same place we were exactly a
    year ago.

Even when we grow.

And yet, "good planning makes it look like you're improvising,"
slowly improving, easing into the easy—concealing the care
taken to seat a throne, love your own, and parent a universe
of ungrateful, unmindful inconsiderates.

The shift from a smile to thoughtfulness is not less
than the gods shapeshifting forms—

swan, bull, shower of gold.

Under the influence of Christianity, the supreme God's image
    was transformed
and Perkunas acquired the position of the Lord of Heaven.

He told you once you had a nice shirt.

No one does.

This Country Will Require You to Be Magical, Then Attempt to Burn You for Being a Witch

Girl-child, power-in-waiting, Revolution,
this world will try to cleave you
in half, reach inside—
lay waste, leave you
a bloody mess of seed,
pulp, carved out meat—
pick your bones
attempt to harness your sweet
for a world full
of eager carrion birds.

Transfigurate:
flower, fruit, fire—
unfurl an inferno
curling coils down
your devil back.
Scorch them with your flame
tongue. Remind them you
predate evangelism;
leave them ashes,
burn them down—
teach them our bodies
are best left alone.

Portrait of a Spirit at Moonlight

I.

Translucent—you are an apparition
as soft as a negligee worn in all
the wrong places and torn in all the right
ways. I've gotten accustomed to men who

are frayed, afraid to leave even as we
heave words like knives to the head knowing
the less-than-labyrinthine path, clearly.
A highway runs past the lie we're living.

We cling closer than two years a-
go when we went whitewater rafting down
winding rapids, laughing and crying.

Then it was good. You smelled of the sweat of
exertion and the tang of lake algae
as I tongued the nook between your neck and
your head and kissed the chin you rested

on me. Remember the old man at the
end of the river? We thought we'd found our
sage until the long trail of his phlegm shot
out and landed at our feet. In disgust

for the next move of the locals, we left.
More mention was made of the symbolism
of his spittle and the brittle vision
of his worn face than the miscarrying

tendency of my ill womb. But we will
agree it is the stress, and not talk of
it, for my own good.

II.

I know you and am still confused by your
dreams. Yet I still kiss you in the moonlight
when you are asleep, determined to keep
sweet memories of you. I watch the way

your eyes light when they're resting on mine
in those fleeting moments when you are fine.
I hear the rustle of sheets as you slowly
creep into bed, excitement flowing from

your fingertips after you've created
and I can't help but recall that this
was once the thrill you'd get from
touching the small of my back.

You are poised for flight,
exodus, escape; I notice you here
fading, slipping, and inexplicably changing
from he that I knew to that which I lack.

After Listening to Whitney Houston's "I Want to Dance with Somebody"

I want to know what happens after the dancing ends.

How the untangling after dawn breaks, goes over.
Lover not named, night fell, and they—came,

answered an insistent call, she hopeful they'll fill
the lonely places with giving and light, warmth.

What happened to Whitney?
The heavy weight of her mother's

expectations, the Church, a pop culture
wanting a princess that can lift every

voice and sing. What Black women do best
is shoulder burden, muling us all to Damascus.

We flicker blue bright and shining, yet burning
too hot inside—learned to save everyone but

ourselves. I just want to dance with somebody.
Exhaustion is inevitable, so I want a combustion

heralded by my own hand. I want to feel the heat
with somebody. Be in a room, spark broke loose,

awaiting a flame,
not just the fire.

We Manage Limited Resources Against Unlimited Needs

so we cleave to one another

        tight as wet clothes
        plastered to damp bodies

we—open hydrants that lift
one another off our feet

choose belief in the enough

        soothe,

press this kiss
into the soft cheek,

        benediction in every breath
        freedom to cry

        into the heft of your chest
        sorrow and sweat

you hold my quivering palm
in your steady hand

        I lean into the precious
        community as contact sport

draw water from communion
full and manifold among the vine,

        care crafted in the creases
        a body composed of globes

sweet skins plump
as summer grapes .

      flush from within
      whole before pressed.

After Listening to Alicia Keys' "When You Really Love Someone"

I never wanted an uncomplicated man,
just the one who'd do anything to have me.

My own Hades.
A man as cool and fresh as autumn air.

One to envelope me in the chill and change,
carry me from light to dark and back again.

A gray sweatpants man, he exuding big
dick energy, his lips, coaxing, enough.

I enjoy flirtation with the dark.

Is there any surprise I enjoy pain with my sex?
Pussy wetter than a slip and slide from punishment.

I crave silkily delivered threats, toothmarks to the throat.
Tying me down electrifies my spine and tingles my toes.

I need the intensity of a lover's attention—a
Hades man's assurances he's thinking of me.

I love the night for its hidden possibilities.

I want to be a worship altar inside someone's home,
draped in desires, token of affections, talismans.

A treasure cradled on the lap he's made a throne.
He holding my hand through heaven and hell.

He the smell of fire during the frost inside
my nose, tangled in my hair and sucking at my ear.

A Hades man, whispering for me to come
back to him soon.

lush and rain, bounty
in lean

We ain't never not been saints

We place our saints on the living
room walls, next to the family pictures.

We can tell you when and how they ascended
to heaven and who wailed

and who wept loudest and longest
and gave the best eulogy.

We get Blessed.

Baptized into wars
that've been fought before—

we hustle hard,
bear crosses,

just want to make mama proud,

become sacrifices,
then martyrs
who die early.

We don't forget

the lost causes
or battles fought.

We love all of them
and who they left behind.

We pour into our half full vessels,
try to fill them up on

hope and honey buns.

We venerate our Fallen

with teddy bears and balloons
tacked to street signs,

t-shirts airbrushed with their faces.
We bulk buy our Shrouds of Turin.

We know a Mother Mary love,
see our charismatic children preach

from the street corners
named for other saints.

The Constant Lesson

My daughter trains to be a ballerina.

The répétiteur leads her through *first and second and third and
    fourth and fifth—*
un, deux, trois, quatre, cinq—hours of technique.

Already she speaks a language I struggle to understand in which she
    finds joy
and thrives.

Her body shaped to bend. [*Plié*. From *plier*.]
What will the world ask her to compromise?

How many ways? To rise. [*Relevé*. From *relever*.] Each lift and strain,
each fall that causes weeping, practice for the moment, she stands
    or leaps

again. To stretch. [*Tendu*. From *étendre*.] She leans into the strain,
    tendons
taut elastic until limber and nimble, contorting and lengthening,
    enthusiastic

and fearless on the street in taking
space. To glide. [*Glissade*. From *glisser*.] Float fly wing baby girl

soar.

Every practice is an exercise in confidence
this overthinking girl transformed

in sweat. Spirit sparkling in communion and discipline
exultant in the mechanics of her form.

I worry.
As she ages will she still—

adore her body,
confide in me,

believe in her magnificence,
and remember there can be beauty in this world?

Bless

Bless the empty streets, the open cul-de-sacs,

      the wide-open possibilities of the abandoned lot,

beauty of glass littered fields grown over, cracks

      exposed for all to see.

Bless the backs and hands of humorous cousins—

      drivers of transit buses trawling the streets, delivering

the other weary machine cog characters to their

      daily destinies.

Bless the edibles man, his cell phone, and all four tires

      of his van, infused with purple urkle and jillybean,

keep him safe and guide him to the drop

      spot.

Bless the roll of fat, supple and rich around our middles

      tattoo across the torso dimpling, a renewed fondness

for molasses and biscuits, coffee, and disinclination

      toward activity.

Small Gifts

I. BAPTISM

At twelve I left home. Began by
packing my trunks—putting away
the things I did not need:

the copper-colored Barbie dolls, the burlap
bag full of half-threaded bobbins, my mother's
hopes and dreams, the once jagged rock

that cut a ragged seam in my back
whose edges I had rubbed smooth.
I was brought to a brick house

bathed in shadow. Seeking protection
I coated my skin in cocoa butter, braided
my coarse curls back into a crown

of nappy ropes, crossed myself three
times, and checked my empty pockets for locks
of my hair I meant to burn so the crows

could not build a nest and drive me crazy,
a packet of salt I stole from the diner
should someone brush my feet with a broom.

Only in hunger did I eat the bread loaf
ends but my purse stayed off the floor. In
the Pentecostal church, another superstition:

they dunk you two times in Baptism waters. Assurance
if the first immersion in the Spirit does not take
accidents happen and you still swallow him whole.

II. SALVATION

I read today that the fourth
of July was once a Black holiday.

After the Civil War, the defeated Confederates—
those traitors—closeted themselves inside

their homes and could not muster the concern
to celebrate liberation from tyranny. They lost

love for their country, so flummoxed
by the notion of independence for us darkies.

Freed Blacks held massive parades to celebrate
the promise of a nation made good.

We met in the public square, the town halls,
arms open wide, whole families lined the streets,

could recite in syncopation—the Declaration
of Independence, the Emancipation Proclamation,

and the Thirteenth Amendment. The lovers
danced the too-la-loo, until their heels hurt

from pounding out their joy, free to link arms,
love in daylight, to raise their own children, to believe

briefly that they were saved.

III. TONGUES

I prepared to receive the message in tongues / tangled mine, with
     twine /

to throttle its tumult / held it taut stilled its flaunt /
flick flutter float and finesse / I said *be still and listen, tongue.*

Lord! I heard you say / where two are gathered in my name /

there I am /

so I gathered them / to my lips / to my kiss / to suckle at each
    breast /
each syllable undulating off the tongue / individual stroke of heat
    / and sleek muscle /

rippled in adoration / twined as a conduit for language /

I sought communion / glorified your name / exaltation: come,
    Savior.

Your name on my tongue / as soft and salt-laden /
as butter pecan ice cream / sipped from your own / mouth.

It was here I heard it—

the hitch in his breathing
when his body broke
cradled in my charcoal,
his musculature in relief

he cried *I knew there was a God*
frame wracked for finding her, in me.

These are the mysteries of my faith

I. CHRIST HAS DIED

[Wo]man is not impervious to Chicago cold.

The vintage walkups with doorjambs
that lean gapped-teeth against the warped
floors necessitate the towel rolled tight
as a blunt forced up against the bottom

of the door. On the windows, the plastic
taped around the seals to catch and blow
back that draft is the same tarp that can
restrain and hide a body (yes, I think it)

every time I call the landlord—
and he pulls his ace card excuses
swears he can't do nothing *the heat*
is as high as it can go unless I raise the rent.

We so accustomed to living on the edge,
we bring out the contraband and grit—
the fuck you mean "the lease say—"
and roll out the space heater from the closet,

share the heated blanket we know better
than to sleep with. We learn to turn
the stove's oven on, let that door hang
open wide to heat the house corners.

We know how to calculate the risk—

it'll either give us release
or burn us to the ground.

II. CHRIST IS RISEN

Big Ma knew how to make a biscuit
light as a cloud, so silky and butter laden
it'd disintegrate like carnival spun
sugar on your tongue.

No one could measure love without the cup
the way she did. Her arthritis-knotted fingers
turning a few handfuls of flour, adding a dash
of baking soda, a pinch of salt, a few lumps
of cold butter; a pour of chilled buttermilk
was just enough to get knuckled under
and transformed into heaven.

She swore that the break between
dusk and dawn was when the best
batch was made, so she woke early,
treated every biscuit as if soufflé.

Each hot mouthful—a perfect hallelujah.
Praise her name.

III. CHRIST WILL COME AGAIN

Here's my secret.
My fingers aren't shaped
for letting go of what is precious to me.
So, when I say, *I just want to be loved like this,*
understand that I mean I want you to take
my pain away. It means I'm telling
you my body is a dry well whimpering
after the next rainfall. That sometimes I just
want to be consoled with familiar comforts:
a three-piece wing fried hard, lemon pepper

seasoning or mild sauce on everything—my fingers
stained sticky red with tang and grease.
But I'm so accustomed to this suffering,
that one night I stood on the curb
in the midst of Chicago's bitter winter
crying without cease or pride
for every inch of you.

Wheel of Fortune

The TV plays a gameshow and my
daughter and I watch a beautiful woman
say she learned to speak English
by watching *Wheel of Fortune*

in her native land. It's a pretty story,
a lie—a good one though.
She's born from colonized country.
and I've walked over those same streets,

felt the paving underneath my soles,
stopped for gas artificially
inflated by British monopoly, asked
for direction and received it easily.

I've ordered fry jacks fresh
out the oil and fire with my boil up.
Eagerly enfolded and embraced
skin folk I barely know.

The diaspora does that—
makes cousins of unknowns.
Our names are on her tongue.
Our tongues know her name.

Should I fault [the flaw in] the story?
[When] I've cooed and exchanged tea
with my tour guide, my thick lips
also thirsting to craft a new autobiography.

How many men have asked
me where I'm from, when
I've only been interested in where
I'm going? Both of us

disappointed, hoping
for what I'm not.
We do what we do to survive.
My mama was braided

into an ancestor's hair.
Me, wombed in the womb
of the wombed.
And when I'm asked my story,

where do I begin—
when the boundaries of
our countries are the lies?
I answer: "lush and rain, bounty

in lean."
I tell them: flowers,
rice and coffee, cotton
and sugar cane.

Tourist, ask me how the same boat
dropped my sister at a different port.
Ask how it felt to finally tongue
the slick flesh of mango.

Ask how the waters of Flint
have touched shores not yet explored.
Tonight, I'm rooting for the liar—
for reinvention and redemption.

I hope she buys a vowel.
Breathless with anticipation,
I await the moment she secures
the bag and says, "just kidding."

All the contestants think
they've figured it out.
But this language is full
of lies too, exceptions and traps.

There needs to be a class
for those of us who learned
words from reading, seeking
and sounding them out.

The ruse is only a success
if she wins. If her tongue
doesn't trip, pray God, Mother
Diaspora, the national narrative

of our *Ragged Dick*—
give a little to get. I've turned
into both child and second
mother, glued to the TV,

dinner fork laden with collard
greens near my lips, shouting
out clues to an unsolved puzzle,
making guesses at what

I don't know. Now my daughter
is me and we're replaying a history
where I pretend I don't know
the answer so she can win too.

Sermon: On the Sanctity of the Beauty Shop

My beautician bends over my back—her fingers flying across my
    tender scalp,
reading my follicles. Said: I need to drink more water, use
    product with less

protein, more time for me—a blind oracle with callouses who
    knows I don't
moisturize as much as I'm supposed to. She's catching every hair
    that's

not ready to be caught snatching and hugging them tight like
    Mary and Magdalene
at the foot of the Cross—that's right, I carry both Blessed
    Mother and Blessed

Apostle in my head, am both, can be easily confused for whore by
    agendaed men
but trust and believe, I deserve the same special handling
    irregardless.

I'm a whole broken woman. And just because I came in one way
don't mean I'm not God-made woman, don't mean I can't be
    transformed, don't

mean I don't sit at the right hand of the Father—look at this
    crown on my head.

You don't have to believe in a higher power to have been taught
    that pain is holy,
that faith, hope, and charity means suspending disbelief and
    venerating lost causes,

just be the woman who loves a man—just be a Black person who
     loves this country,
just plant a garden and watch it grow, then winter and frost, see
     what grows back in

better yet just birth a Black child and pray that they live.

My beautician's the only one who asks what I want. I say in return
     give me a protective
styling, remind me of my mother's thighs bracketing my shoulders,
     Blue Magic,

and cocoa butter, Wild Growth, Mane 'n Tail, Luster's." I'm tired
     of what makes
me stronger. Sometimes I want to be as weak and fragile as my
     follicles.

Can you please hold my hand for just a second? Ask me: *Girl, you ok?*
Lay my baby hairs with edge control and say: *I've been thinking*
     about you.

Black Bodies

College-kid-bold-nappy-headed Black
wearing "I am a Chemist. Save effort and assume I am right"
black shirt white lettering
deep Black.

/

Sitting outside
I order the kale and quinoa,
lightly dressed in black
pepper, a yogurt Caesar,
steak seared black on the outside,
medium rare in the center
I eat at the wrought iron café
table under the awning,
awing the Black folks
who walk by.
They head nod front to back
to acknowledge my Black
face kissed by sun rays.

/

We Black folks' secret decoder ring.
In fact, my phone call with East Coast sings
with the equivalent of Black jive,
so Black
we debate the deliciousness
of banana pudding with Nilla
versus Chessmen.

/
Yo-mama-so Black Black.
Blacker than a youthful heart attack Black
that use the-White-voice-at-the-job-Black
that knick-knack-paddy-whack Black
that big Black, little Black, get-it-from-her-mama-Black
just-like-your-daddy-Black,
that listening to Black on Both Sides Black,
likely-to-be-shot-in-the-back-Black
talented tenth Black, *I have a Dream* Black
pound cake Black, Pan African Black,
bitch Black, nigger Black, nigga Black,
nerd Black, blues Black, talk-back Black,
block-running Black, money-chasing Black,
book-read Black, bad-bitch Black,
bougie-Black, jezebel and mammy Black,
the-conscientious-of-optics Black, all
trying-to-get-by-Black

/
skillet Black
sienna Black
redbone Black,
high yellow Black,
snow white Black

/
untreated mental trauma Black
take it to the Father Black
holding space for you Black

Love Letter to The Revolution No. 2

Sweets,

When I was a child, my mother and aunts would sit in the kitchen

gossiping—bathed in moonlight, *diffused through*—a dream,
    wine, religion, and success.

I hold the stars between my teeth—your tumults, your marriages,
    aches, and your deaths—to fashion a world that will hold all
    the promised to come,

in her outstretched palm. I'll teach you a poem: *show me someone*
    not full of herself and I'll show
you a hungry person.

Drink: laugh and dance and sing and play.

If you don't look back, the future never happens.

Where   are   we   going,   without   you?

Notes

"Love Letter to The Revolution No. 1"

"Little Sister" is from "Appalachian Elegy" by bell hooks

"Nobody spoke to me about the moon" is from "Senses of Heritage" by Ntozake Shange

"to fashion a world that will hold all the people" is from "For My People" by Margaret Walker

"these stains & scars are mine" is from "nappy edges (a cross country sojourn)" by Ntozake Shange

"I will give you thunder / shatter your hearts / with rain / let snow soothe you / make your // healing water / clear sweet" is from "Appalachian Elegy" by bell hooks

"laugh and dance and sing and / play and drink / their wine and religion and success" is from "For My People" by Margaret Walker

"Come celebrate / with me that everyday / something has tried to kill me / and has failed" is from "won't you celebrate with me" by Lucille Clifton

"Be who you are and will be / learn to cherish / that boisterous Black Angel that drives you" is from "For Each of You" by Audre Lorde

"Picture the daylight / bringing her to woods // full of birth moons" is from "Haiku and Tanka for Harriet Tubman" by Sonia Sanchez

84

"Love Letter to the Revolution No. 2"

"Sweets" is from "the mother" by Gwendolyn Brooks

"When I was a child, my mother and aunts would sit in the
     kitchen // gossiping. . . ." is from "The blessed angels" by Toi
     Derricotte

"bathed in moonlight *diffused through*" is from "Mothers" by
Nikki Giovanni

"wine, religion, and success" is from "For My People" by
     Margaret Walker

"I hold the stars between my teeth" is from "14 haiku" by Sonia
     Sanchez

"tumults, your marriages, aches, and your deaths" is from "For
     My People" by Margaret Walker

"to fashion a world that will hold all" is from "For My People" by
     Margaret Walker

"the promised to come" is from "Mothers" by Nikki Giovanni

"in her outstretched palm" is from "I Have Been a Stranger in a
     Strange Land" by Rita Dove

"I'll teach you a poem" is from "Mothers" by Nikki Giovanni

*"show me someone not full of herself and I'll show / you a hungry
     person"* is from "Poem for a Lady Whose Voice I Like" by
     Nikki Giovanni

"laugh and dance and sing and play" is from "For My People" by
     Margaret Walker

"If you don't look back, the future never happens" is from "Dawn
     Revisited" by Rita Dove

Acknowledgments

Grateful acknowledgment is made to the editors of the following journals and magazines in which these poems first appeared, sometimes in different versions:

The Adirondack Review: "Mame Coumba Bang Speaks to The Revolution"

Anomaly: Online Journal of International Literature and Art: "Full Throated"

Cave Wall: "Sister/Seraphim, Inextinguishable Light" and "These are the mysteries of my faith"

The Journal: "Love Letter to The Revolution No. 1" and "Love Letter to The Revolution No. 2"

Junto Magazine: "Because You Need to Learn" (as "where I, the poet, start with a form but the memories break it / me apart")

The Midwest Quarterly: "Portrait of a Spirit at Moonlight" (as "In Moonlight, Semi-Transparent") and "Till it Moves Like a Slow Song Sounds"

Mom Egg Review: "We Manage Limited Resources Against Unlimited Needs"

Mortar Magazine: "Dust to Bones"

Negative Capability Press: "Aide-Memoire" and "If you've ever been to a Pentecostal tent revival, then you know"

Obsidian: Literature & Arts in the African Diaspora: "Small Gifts"

Psaltery & Lyre: "My Mama's Got Her GED in Existentialism and Human Emotion"

Rise Up Review: "Pyriscence" and "Transfiguration, or As the Spirit Is, So Follows the Body"

So to Speak: feminist journal of language and art: "Black Marie-Antoinette"

Sugar House Review: "Kink Therapy, or An Alternate History of the World"

SWWIM Every Day: "This Country Will Require You to Be Magical, Then Attempt to Burn You for Being a Witch"

The Texas Review: "After Listening to Alicia Keys' 'When You Really Love Someone,'" "After Listening to Megan Thee Stallion's 'Thot Shit,'" "After Listening to Roberta Flack Singing 'Angelitos Negros,'" and "After Listening to Whitney Houston's 'I Want to Dance with Somebody'"

VIDA Review: "Black Bodies" and "Sermon: On the Sanctity of the Beauty Shop"

Yemassee Journal: "A Mouth Full of Prayers for Wendy Williams"

A lot of individuals were instrumental in the making of *Seraphim* and it wouldn't be complete without thanking them for the life, love, energy, time, space, support, and/or feedback they've provided toward this endeavor.

First, my daughter Ella Fair-Marie Zobitz who I have the joy of nurturing—I'm humbled to be your parent. You inspire me daily to build a world that will hold all the people. Mike Zobitz who encouraged me to begin writing again and then created the space for it to happen.

Katrina Page, thank you for gifting me this world and the will to thrive in it. To the incredible village of mothers and aunties who have loved and nurtured me over my long life—thank you for teaching me joy.

Thank you to Sherine Gilmour for being the best manuscript partner.

Thank you to the poet mothers who've inspired my journey: bell hooks, Maya Angelou, Rita Dove, Audre Lorde, Ntozake Shange, Margaret Walker, Lucille Clifton, Sonia Sanchez, Gwendolyn Brooks, Alice Walker, Nikki Giovanni, Toi Derricotte, Toni Cade Bambara, Patricia Smith—the list is longer than I can type because great is the legacy I've received. Thanks to all the ancestors and their voices.

Thank you to Vainis Aleksa and to Simone Muench for recognizing my passion for poetry and gifting me rigor.

Thank you to the CavanKerry Press team—Gabriel Cleveland, John Cusack Handler, Dana Harris-Trovato, Dimitri Reyes, Tamara Al-Qaisi-Coleman, Joy Arbor, Ryan Scheife, and Baron Wormser.

Seraphim wouldn't be what it is without all of you. Thank you for your time, trust, and energy.

Thank you to all the Black womxn and girls who make the world such a vibrant, interesting, and joy-filled place in the midst of—everything.

CavanKerry's Mission

A not-for-profit literary press serving art and community, Cavan-Kerry is committed to expanding the reach of poetry and other fine literature to a general readership by publishing works that explore the emotional and psychological landscapes of everyday life, and to bringing that art to the underserved where they live, work, and receive services.

Other Books in the Emerging Voices Series

This book was printed on paper from responsible sources.

Seraphim was typeset in Garamond Premier Pro by Adobe senior type designer Robert Slimbach. It is a practical, 21st-century update to Claude Garamond's metal punches and book types originally created in the mid-1500s, considered to be the pinnacle of beauty and practicality in typefounding.